The Simply Romantic Husband

150 Fun and Creative Ways to Romance Your Wife

Honor Books
Tulsa, Oklahoma

The Simply Romantic Husband:
150 Fun and Creative Ways to Romance Your Wife
ISBN 1-56292-928-3
Copyright ©2000 by Campus Crusade for Christ, Inc.
doing business as FamilyLife
3900 North Rodney Parham Road
Little Rock, AR 72212

Published by Honor Books
P.O. Box 55388
Tulsa, OK 74155

Compiled and edited by Leslie J. Barner

Foreword

Remember when . . . you saw that sparkle in her eyes every time you surprised her with a bouquet of flowers? Remember the love letters you wrote, that caused her to giggle and her heart to flutter? Or the times you lovingly gazed into her eyes from across the table at a romantic restaurant? The smile on her face was priceless. Yesterday's memories can be today's reality with this collection of ideas and suggestions, designed to help you create a more romantic marriage.

Romance is not the foundation of marriage, but romance helps couples refresh their relationship, renew their friendship, and delight in one another. Every marriage needs to have the pleasurable feelings of romance to thrive and grow. Think back in your relationship. Hold hands, embrace, and stroll arm in arm, just as you did when you were dating. Rekindling the romance in your marriage doesn't require a lot of time and money. All you need is a willing heart and the commitment to do it.

The FamilyLife speaker team has provided you with some of their best romance-building ideas—tried and proven in their own homes. Use them to spice up your marriage with a little romance. Adapt them as necessary to suit your own circumstances and personalities. Let them spark some creative ideas of your own! Become a student of your wife. Observe her, talk with her, discover what she really likes, things she considers romantic. Most of all, find out what you can do to make her feel more loved, appreciated, and valued. Your wife will be blessed and encouraged, you will be her knight in shining armor, and your marriage will grow in love, friendship, and passion!

Dennis and Barbara Rainey
Dennis Rainey is the executive director of FamilyLife and father of six.
Barbara Rainey is co-founder of FamilyLife and mother of six.

Ways to Romance Your Wife:

Questions to Stimulate Intimate Conversations

1.

What is the most romantic thing

I could ever do for you?

2.

What kind of
friend do you most
need me to be?

3.

What would you consider

the ideal marriage?

How can we work toward it?

4.

What has God been teaching you lately?

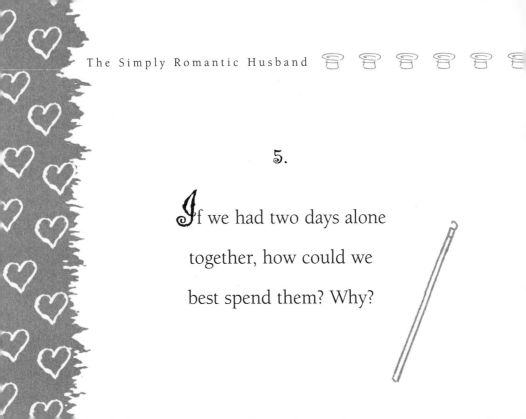

5.

*I*f we had two days alone
together, how could we
best spend them? Why?

6.

If we could go anywhere

in the world together,

where would we go? Why?

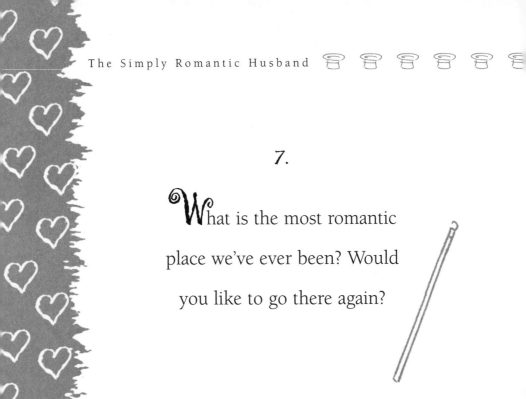

7.

What is the most romantic place we've ever been? Would you like to go there again?

8.

What three

dates would you consider

our most romantic?

9.

On a scale of 1 to 10, how would

you rate the quality of our

time together? Why?

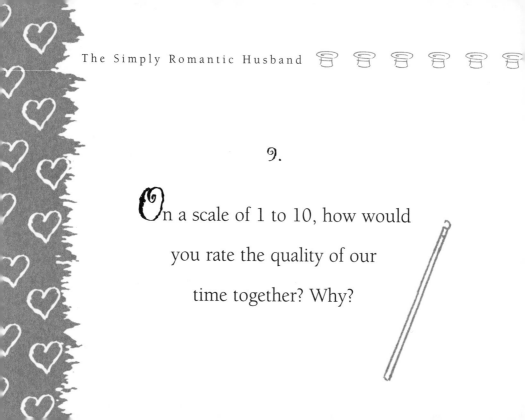

10.

What can I do to really

understand how you're feeling?

11.

What could I do to best help

you in the next week?

12.

If you could change anything
about the way I treat you,
what would it be?

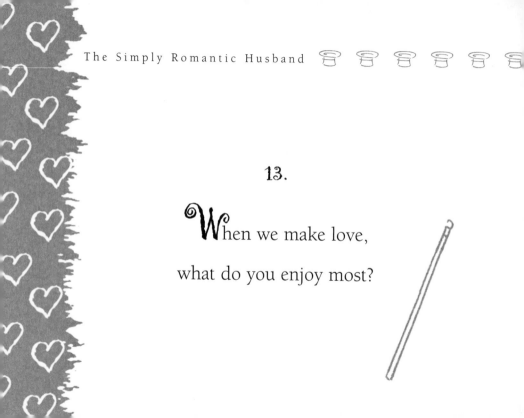

13.

When we make love,

what do you enjoy most?

14.

What do I do
that really makes you
feel loved? In what ways can
I make you feel more loved?

15.

*I*f I could help you fulfill your wildest dream, what would you want me to do?

16.

If I were an animal,

what kind would I be? Why?

17.

What about my personality

do you like most?

18.
What part of my face
do you like most?

19.
What part of my physique
do you like most?

20.

What Bible character do

I remind you of? Why?

21.

What do you want our family

to be remembered for?

22.

How am I doing at fatherhood?

In what ways can I improve?

23.

How are we doing at dealing with conflict

in our home? How can we improve?

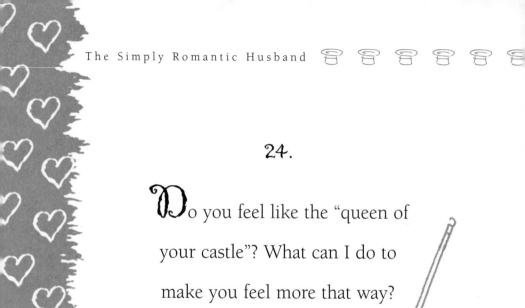

24.

Do you feel like the "queen of your castle"? What can I do to make you feel more that way?

25.

What is the funniest or most embarrassing thing that has ever happened to us (a time when we laughed really hard together)?

26.

What do you miss most about your childhood and/or teenage years?

27.

Who was your favorite teacher? What did you learn from him or her?

28.

What do we want our life

to be like in 10 years?

29.

If you were to take your first name

and make an acrostic describing your life's

purpose, what would each letter represent?

30.

What are three things that I say or do that make you feel close to me? What are three things that I say or do that distance you from me?

31.

What are two of your lifelong dreams and what progress have you made toward fulfilling them? How can I help you?

32.

What three ingredients are a

must for a romantic evening?

33.

ow can I be more helpful

around the house?

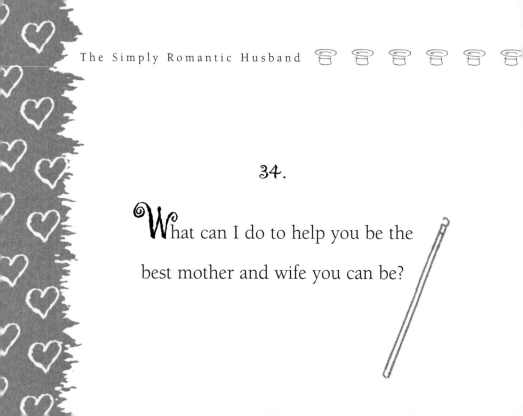

34.

What can I do to help you be the

best mother and wife you can be?

Ways to Romance Your Wife:

Romantic Gestures

35.

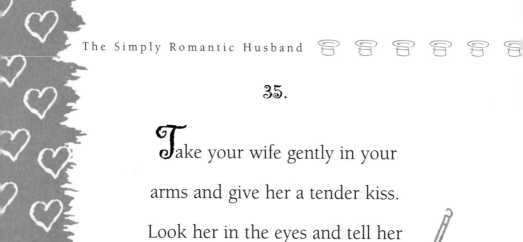

Take your wife gently in your arms and give her a tender kiss. Look her in the eyes and tell her you love her very much and you'd marry her all over again!

36.

Fix your wife her favorite breakfast in bed,

then wake her up with a kiss.

Sit in a chair by the bed and

talk with her while she eats.

37.

Tell your wife that being close

to her still excites you.

38.

Volunteer to pick up

the dry cleaning.

39.

Have a bubble bath and her favorite music or book ready for her after an especially hard day. Give her a massage. Then, let her go to sleep.

40.

Write a letter to your wife

describing her strengths

and your need for her.

41.

$\mathcal{F}$or Valentine's Day, buy a pad of

post-it notes and write a brief

message to your wife on each page.

Hide them in different places

where she will find them.

42.

Encourage her with some scripture you think describes her walk with God. For example, if you are impressed by her humble heart, read Philippians 2:1-11.

43.

In front of a gathering of people—
perhaps at a family reunion, at work,
or at a party—praise your wife,
saying how much you love and
appreciate her. Be specific.

44.

One Saturday morning, tell your wife that she is "queen for a day." Handle all her household responsibilities—cleaning, cooking, taking care of the kids, etc. Let her spend her day as she chooses.

45.

Take a walk in the rain holding hands.

Stop at each stop sign or crossroads and

kiss her and tell her something

you like about her.

46.

On Labor Day, clean the house

for your wife.

47.

Make a commitment to pray with
your wife for a few minutes every night
before you go to bed. Keep track of
how God answers your prayers.

48.

Schedule a weekly devotional time with

your wife. Take some time to read through

Scripture, talk about how it applies

to your lives, and pray together.

49.

Hide chocolate kisses around the

house and write her a note that says,

"A kiss for a kiss." Then every

time she finds a hidden kiss,

give her one of yours!

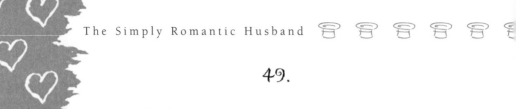

50.

At the first signs of Spring, plant a bed of flowers before she gets to it herself. Stake it with a love note.

51.

$\mathfrak{D}$o a project around the house that has been on the "back burner."

52.

$\mathcal{L}$eave a big note on the
washing machine thanking her
for washing your clothes.

53.

*L*eave a single rose (of a unique color)

with a love note (telling her how special

she is to you) where she can find it

after you've left for work.

54.

Draw a bubble bath for two.

(Set up the bathroom ahead of time

with extra plants from other rooms,

lit candles, and soft music.)

55.

*P*lan and cook dinner one evening

to give her a night off.

56.

raise her in front of the

children about the things she

does, the way she cooks, etc.

57.

Wash her feet and give
her a complete pedicure,
including a foot massage.

58.

Phone her every day for one week
and describe a part of her body that
you like, and why; or a spiritual quality she
possesses, and how she demonstrates it
(each day choosing a different quality or part).

59.

Get up before your wife

one weekday morning and

wake her with her favorite

morning beverage and a kiss.

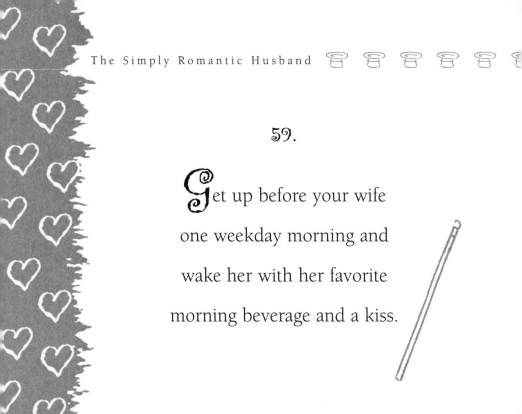

60.

Write special notes of love and appreciation and hide them in places where your wife will eventually find them (i.e., dresser drawers, books she is reading, the microwave, her jewelry box, etc.).

61.

Be a gentleman:
open doors for her, open her car door,
pull out her chair, offer your hand
while walking, and put your arm
around her when standing.

62.

*P*hone her once a day to say,

"I'm thinking of you. . . ."

63.

While you're away on a business trip,

have a bouquet of flowers delivered

to your wife with a romantic note that

says something like, "I can't wait

to get back home to you. . . ."

64.

Surprise her by coming home
from a business trip a day earlier
than she expects, then spend
the day with her.

65.

*P*eriodically, mail her a romantic card or love letter.

66.

*E*ncourage her by helping
her fold the laundry or
wash the dishes.

67.

*T*ake a short evening stroll together after
dinner every day.

(You may want to ask the kids to join you.)

68.

Set aside a special day to spend time
alone with the kids, once a week,
every other week, or once a month,
so your wife can go shopping and run
errands alone or with a girlfriend.
Perhaps she can use some quiet
time alone at home, and you
can take the kids out for
lunch and a movie.

Ways to Romance Your Wife:

Ideas for Romantic Dates

69.

Take your wife shopping and express
interest in what she's looking at.
Be patient! Enjoy your time with her.

70.

Plan a romantic evening:
Dine at a nice restaurant and
then go to the theater or ballet.

71.

Arrange for your friends to make dinner,

create a romantic atmosphere, and serve you.

(Hire a violinist or harpist from the local university

or church for an added touch of romance!)

72.

Take a hot air balloon ride,
go horseback riding, or just
watch the sunset together.

73.

Take your wife on a romantic dinner

cruise—or just go on a walk together

for 30-45 minutes—and share

your dreams with one another.

74.

Surprise your wife by taking her

to an outdoor café for brunch.

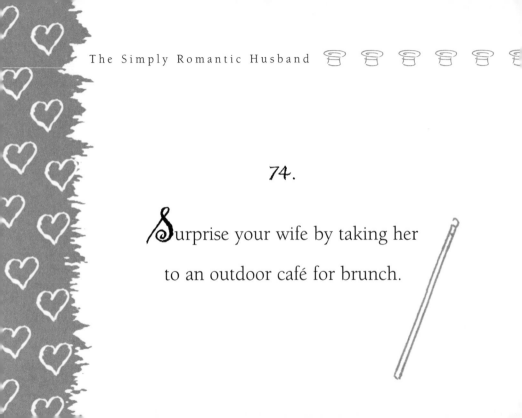

75.

Go out for ice cream
and let her pick the topics
of conversation.

76.

Rent a limousine, and have
dinner in the limo while
the driver tours the town.

77.

Create a romantic setting with candles
and sparkling grape juice, and watch
a romantic movie together.

78.

Spend an evening at home
looking at old scrapbooks,
listening to her favorite kind
of music, and dancing.

79.

Prepare your wife's favorite meal,
eat by candlelight, then relax in front
of the fireplace with some soft music.

80.

Write her a romantic poem,

then take her to the park

and read it to her.

81.

$\mathcal{T}$ake her out to breakfast,
lunch, and dinner
all in the same day!

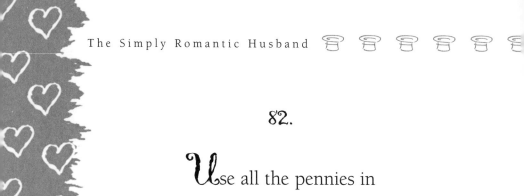

82.

Use all the pennies in

your piggy bank for a date.

Don't spend any other money.

See how creative you can be!

83.

Go for a long walk or a bike ride

(2-3 hours), stopping

for lunch together.

84.

Hang out at the

flea market together.

85.

Arrange for a sitter outside of your home.

Have a romantic dinner delivered

to the house with a candlelit table

for two, and have soft music playing.

(If your budget allows, hire a musician!)

86.

Go out for an early game of tennis,

miniature golf, bowling, or

some other activity, then have

dinner at an outdoor café.

87.

Buy, rent, or borrow a tripod and take silly pictures together at a park. Get the pictures developed at a one-hour photo shop, and enjoy them over lunch or dinner at a restaurant.

88.

Drive out to the mountains
for a hike or take a walk around
the lake, then ask the locals
where they like to eat.

89.

Go for a long, brisk walk together

and end up at a deli for sandwiches.

Then stroll home together hand in hand.

90.

Set up a candlelit dinner in your
own backyard. Wear formal attire,
and play soft music.

91.

Take a carryout dinner
and candles to a pool. Go for
a late night swim.

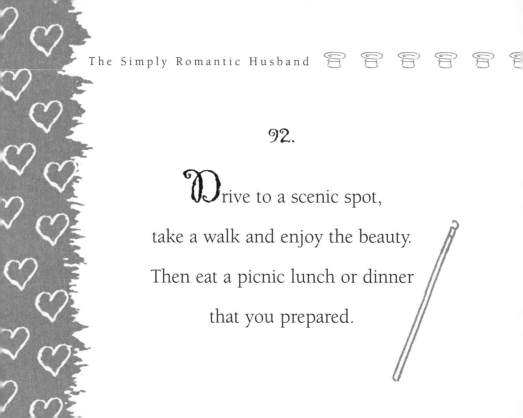

92.

Drive to a scenic spot,

take a walk and enjoy the beauty.

Then eat a picnic lunch or dinner

that you prepared.

93.

𝒫lan and prepare dinner
(make it simple if necessary),
then serve it either on the patio,
or in the bedroom, and talk
only about intimate things.

(See: Questions to Stimulate Intimate Conversations.)

94.

Check out a book of love poems from your local library, and take your wife to a local lake or park at dawn, or dusk, and read selected poems to her.

95.

Dress up like a fancy restaurant waiter,

and serve your wife dinner at a candlelit

table for two (the food could be carry-out

from her favorite restaurant), then

go change and be her date.

96.

Take her out to an early dinner,

then go for a stroll together

in the mall.

97.

Take her on a "Scavenger Hunt Date"!
Give her the challenge of going with you
to the mall and buying 10 small items
with only a small, set amount of money
to spend (i.e., $3.72), then take her
to a nice restaurant.

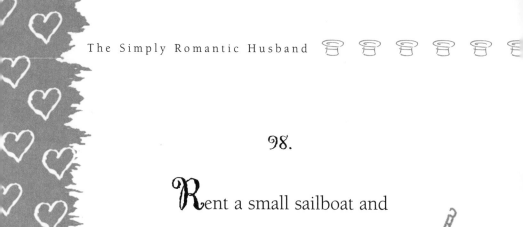

98.

ℛent a small sailboat and
sail out on a lake to watch
the sunrise or sunset.

99.

Pack a picnic dinner and pictures of your past years together. Drive to a nearby park or lake and reminisce.

100.

Court her again by recreating
something fun you did when
you first dated one another.

Ways to Romance Your Wife:

Romantic Gift Ideas

101.

Buy a book of love poems

and read a special poem

to her every night.

102.

Give your wife a "Day of Beauty" package.
Arrange for her to have a facial, makeover,
manicure, pedicure, and/or her hair cut,
colored, and styled. Choose some or all!

103.

Buy a basket and fill it with sweet things for your sweetheart (for example: love notes, chocolates, jams, lollipops, heart-shaped candles, perfume, etc.).

104.

Pick some spring flowers
and give them to your wife
with a sweet note.

105.

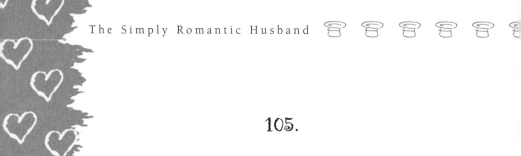

Buy your wife a bottle of her favorite

perfume and present it to her

with a romantic card.

106.

Buy your wife a special nightgown

or pajamas—the kind she

most likes to wear.

107.

*G*ive your wife a homemade coupon
booklet consisting of romantic and
practical "freebies" (i.e., "Redeem
this coupon for a free foot massage" or,
"This coupon good for one free evening out
with your friends while I watch the kids.").
Include a blank one for her to
fill in whatever she wants.

108.

Gather pictures from your years

together, make a special album,

and present it to her.

109.

Create a handmade greeting card

praising your wife.

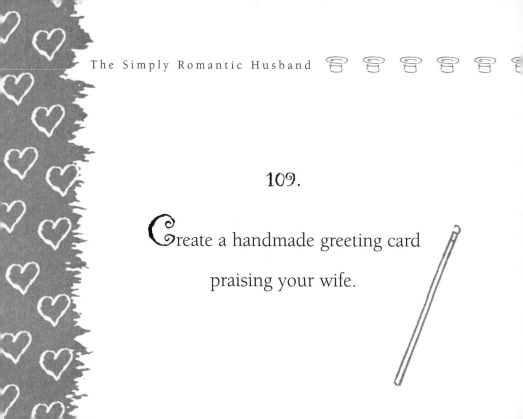

110.

Purchase her a new book by her favorite author, and sign the inside beginning with the words "Just because."

111.

Buy your wife a

special piece of jewelry.

(Maybe even design it yourself!)

112.

Put an advertisement in the
newspaper to tell your wife you're still in
love with her. Or make a mini-paper
of your own on the computer!

113.

*L*eave your wife a long-stemmed

red rose in her car one morning,

with a small note that simply says,

"I love you."

114.

Create a special Thanksgiving Book and through words and pictures, list all the reasons you are thankful for her.

115.

Buy your wife a new dress

or outfit for the holidays.

116.

Hire a maid to clean the house right before the most stressful part of the holidays.

117.

$\mathcal{G}$ive her a coupon book to her

favorite fast-food restaurant

with a note that says,

"For your use only!"

118.

Surprise her one evening

by bringing home her favorite dessert

from her favorite restaurant.

119.

Give her a gift certificate

to a bath and body shop.

Offer to watch the kids so she

can go to the mall to redeem it.

120.

Give her a set amount of money (can be $20 or more) and chauffeur her around to garage sales one Saturday morning, then take her to brunch.

121.

Buy a beautiful flower vase at a

reasonable price, and fill it with flowers

(from your garden, grocery store, or florist)

on a regular basis.

122.

Get her a gift certificate to her favorite store and hide it under her pillow, or somewhere she will discover it.

123.

Wrap her favorite candy bar or pastry in a new piece of lingerie, with a note telling her how sweet she is.

124.

Arrange ahead of time with the waiter

at her favorite breakfast restaurant to have

a small gift (jewelry, gift certificate,

music tape, etc.) served on her

pancakes or waffles, as the topping.

125.

Surprise her with chocolates on
her pillow, hot coffee in the cupboard,
or jewelry under her pillow, with
a note that says something like,
"I'm so glad to be back home
with you." after you've
returned from a business trip.

126.

When you go away on a business trip,

mail her a postcard, letter, or card

from the airport or, upon

arrival at your destination.

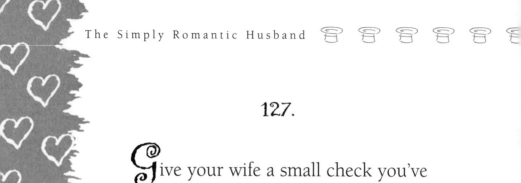

127.

Give your wife a small check you've

received (honorarium, bonus, rebate, etc.)

and sign it over to her to spend

any way she desires.

128.

Have a special gift basket made for your wife. It can be for her personally (perfume, bubble bath, shower gel, scented soap, etc.) or for the two of you to use together (two glasses, a bottle of sparkling cider, scented candles, scented body oil, etc.)

129.

Give her lingerie wrapped and
placed in memory boxes,
with a note sharing a special
romantic memory in each box
(memory boxes are sold at
most craft stores).

130.

Put together a memory album

with love letters from a

specific year or several years.

Categorize them and use clip art.

131.

*P*resent her a "Journal of My Love
for You"—a journal that you fill
with dated love letters written to
your wife over a period of time.

Ways to Romance Your Wife:

Romantic Getaways

132.
Choose the most special part of
your honeymoon and recreate
it on a smaller scale.

133.
Take your wife to a nice hotel
with a heated pool, in the desert,
in the middle of winter, to enjoy
a special time of romance
and a break from the cold.

134.

Arrange a surprise getaway weekend for the two of you. Have her bags packed and in the trunk of the car, and arrange for a baby sitter in advance. Take Friday off from work, and treat your wife to breakfast. Arrange for the waiter to deliver a note to your wife during breakfast announcing that you are whisking her away for a weekend of romance and passion.

135.

During the winter,
make reservations at a local hotel
that has an indoor pool and hot tub.
Check in as early as possible and relax
together around the pool. Sleep in
the next morning, and enjoy
a light breakfast in your room.

136.

Rent a condominium or beach house

with a view. Take long walks along the shore,

and be sure to enjoy the sunset and/or

sunrise together during your stay.

137.

Take your wife on a fall trip to an Amish county. Stay at a bed and breakfast. Try to plan your trip during a craft fair, and take her shopping for antiques.

138.

Go back to a place you went when
you were newlyweds and stay overnight.
Be sure to bring pictures from that time
and take a romantic trip down
memory lane together.

139.

*S*ave up enough money

to surprise her with an

economical, but exotic cruise

for 4 days and 3 nights!

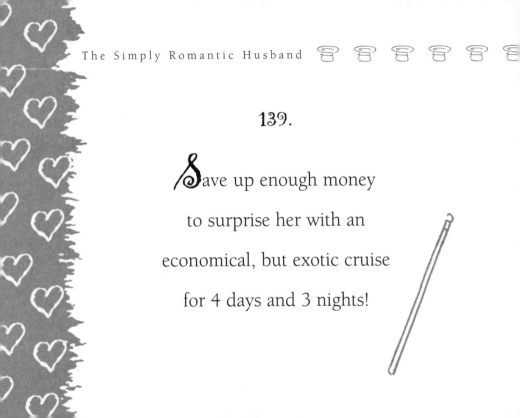

140.

Make weekend arrangements for your children, pack bags for the two of you, and ask the sitter to arrive at the same time you plan to kidnap your wife. Then, take her to a surprise destination that will include a weekend stay at a nice hotel and tickets to a stage play or concert.

141.

ℛent or borrow an R.V.

and take her on a scenic

road trip for a few days

(without the kids).

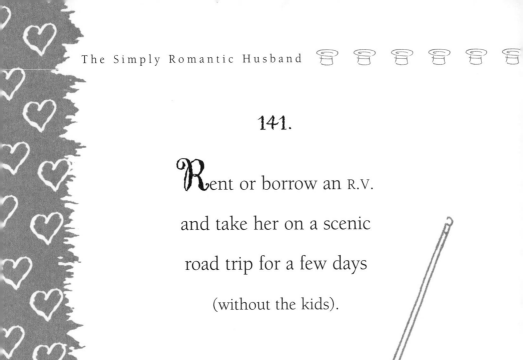

142.

Secretly pack her clothes.

Then, one ordinary Sunday after church,

take her to dinner far away from

home and to stay overnight at a

hotel or bed and breakfast.

143.

Every evening for a week, leave a card on her pillow with clues leading up to a surprise weekend getaway.

144.

Take your wife for an overnight
camp-out in your backyard.
Share the same sleeping bag and have
a Bible study by candlelight or flashlight—
about Adam and Eve in the garden. The meal
for the evening should be fruit salad.

145.

Take her for an overnight stay at a beach-front hotel. Get a room with a balcony and a view of the ocean. Have dinner delivered to your room, and enjoy candlelit dining on your balcony in formal attire. Time your dinner to be eaten during sunset. Then take an evening stroll on the beach in bare feet.

146.

Rent or borrow a mountain cabin (near an outlet center), and let her shop 'til she drops. Then take her out for dinner, rent videos, and sleep in the next day.

147.

Take your wife on a surprise trip to a bed and breakfast in a romantic setting. Go on Friday night and enjoy a romantic evening with dinner, soft music, and slow dancing. On Saturday, after a hearty breakfast, spend the day setting and reviewing goals (family, marital, personal, spiritual, business, etc.) and planning your calendars for the next six months. Then on Sunday, worship the Lord and pray together, communicating with the Lord about your plans and goals.

148.

Take your wife to a resort

where she will be pampered.

Make sure there is a hot tub

in the bedroom.

149.

Save up money for a moderate vacation
that requires air travel. Give the money
to your closest friends asking them to
make flight and hotel arrangements
for a surprise destination in the USA.
Have them take you to the airport,
escort you to the ticket counter,
and disclose where you and your
wife will be going together!

150.

Have dinner at a

special restaurant and plan

your next getaway!

About the Authors...

The FamilyLife Marriage Conference speaker team is a dynamic, fun-filled group of people who are committed to encouraging and equipping couples to build strong marriages and godly homes. They are authors, teachers, ministers, executives, psychologists, marriage counselors, athletes, and business owners. They are also husbands, wives, fathers, and mothers—people just like you.

Though the speakers have varying backgrounds, each one has gained in-depth, real-life experience and education in the area of marriage and family.

At the FamilyLife Marriage Conferences, the speakers' presentations are biblically and professionally sound, and are designed to provide you with:

- Practical tools to strengthen and build your relationship

- Ways to open the channels of communication

- Creative methods to resolve conflict in your home

- Opportunities to bring you closer to your mate and your children

For many couples, the conference is a romantic getaway, or a time to draw closer to each other and to the Lord; for others it may help to save their marriage and family. But for all, the FamilyLife Marriage Conference is a "Weekend to Remember!"

If you would like more information on the FamilyLife Marriage or FamilyLife Parenting Conferences, please call 1-800-FL-TODAY.

The following couples comprise the speaker teams and were the contributors of these simply great ideas:

Barry & Pam Abell, Jose & Michelle Alvarez II, James & Anne Arkins, Bruce & Julie Boyd, Charles & Karen Boyd, Dan & Julie Brenton, Karl & Junanne Clauson, Doug & Patty Daily, Kyle & Sharon Dodd, Tim & Joy Downs, Don & Suzanne Dudgeon, Michael & Cindy Easley, Dennis & Jill Eenigenburg, Tom & Toni Fortson, Jerry & Nancy Foster, James & Cynthia Gorton, Floyd & Diana Green, Dick & Nancy Hastings, Howard & Jeanne Hendricks, David & Sharon Hersh, Bruce & Janet Hess, Alan & Theda Hlavka, Bob & Jan Horner, Joel & Cindy Housholder, Bill & Terri Howard, Don & Suzanne Hudson, Dan & Kathie Jarrell, Ron & Mary Jenson, Dave & Peggy Jones, Jim & Renee Keller, Tim & Darcy Kimmel, Bob & Mary Ann Lepine, Crawford & Karen Loritts, Ray & Robyn McKelvy, Tim & Noreen Muehlhoff, Bill & Pam Mutz, Johnny & Lezlyn Parker, Tom & Brenda Preston, Dick & Paula Purnell, Dennis & Barbara Rainey, Gary & Barbara Rosberg, Steve & Debbie Schall, Mark & Lisa Schatzman, Jeff & Brenda Schulte, Chuck & Beth Simmons, Greg & Bonnie Speck, Gary & Luci Stanley, Dave & Sande Sunde, Rick & Judy Taylor, Roger & Joanne Thompson, J.T. & Enid Walker, John & Linda Willett, Dave & Ann Wilson, Jerry & Sheryl Wunder, John & Susan Yates, Mick & Helen Yoder,

Special thanks to Lesie Barner for compiling and editing these ideas.

Additional copies of this book are available from your local bookstore.

If you have enjoyed this book, or if it has
impacted your life, we would like to hear from you.
Please contact us at:

Honor Books
Department E
P.O. Box 55388
Tulsa, Oklahoma 74155

Or by e-mail at info@honorbooks.com

Honor Books
Tulsa, Oklahoma